WHY SHOULD I SPEAK IN TONGUES?

Dr. David R. Chisholm

ISBN: 1463677863
ISBN-13:9781463677862

DEDICATION

I would like to dedicate this book to my wife, Kyong, and my three beautiful daughters: Nicole, Janelle, and Jamie. They have followed my faith throughout the years into some *treacherous waters* and never really questioned, "Is Dad really hearing from God?" They have forsaken all to follow Him more than once, and they trusted my judgment in leading our family. Thanks for believing in the call on my life!

CONTENTS

ACKNOWLEDGMENTS

There are two men who have served as spiritual leaders in my life and who I would like to acknowledge in this book: Dr. Robert Nichols of Ft. Worth, Texas, who has served as my Pastor since 1982, and Prophet Kevin Leal of Pensacola, Florida, who has been my assigned Prophet for many years. Thank you for being faithful leaders in my life. Your character and wisdom have been instrumental in my life and the development of my calling. Thanks to all those who helped me edit and finish this book and to Derick Midcap for the cover design. And to all the leaders of the Rock Churches for your tireless effort to lead our congregations into the fullness of God: You Rock!

1
MY QUEST

"Brother Dave, look what I found in the Book of Mark!" I exclaimed as I stood before the pastor of Bethel Baptist Church. It was after the Sunday morning service, and I was so excited about a passage I had discovered while reading the Bible. "It says that the people who believe in Jesus can cast out devils and speak in tongues and heal the sick and…"

"Now, Dave," Pastor Dave said, "you need to understand that these things passed away after Paul died."

"Where does it say that?" I asked, sincerely wanting to understand.

"In 1 Corinthians chapter 13, Dave. It says after that which is perfect has come, that which is in part shall be done away with. Whether there be tongues they shall cease."

"Well, what has come since Paul died?" I asked.

The Pastor's face changed. Obviously frustrated with my inquisition, he said sternly, "Now, Dave, Jesus didn't speak in tongues, Paul didn't speak in tongues, I don't speak in tongues, and you don't need to speak in tongues! We have the Bible today, and we don't need those things!"

"Paul wrote the Bible, and he needed them," I said, half under my breath, as I turned to walk away. It was clear that this conversation was over, and I had just been admonished. I felt both confused and frustrated, but I knew what I had read, and the Bible said *these signs will follow them that believe.*

"Well, back to my Bible," I thought.

When I went home, I continued to read and moved into what I call the censored section of the Bible: 1 Corinthians, Chapters 12 - 14. As I was reading, I found the following scripture:

"I thank my God I speak with tongues more than you all; yet in the church I would rather speak five words with my understanding, that I may teach others also, than ten thousand words in a tongue." 1 Corinthians 14:18-19

What? I thought, *Paul spoke in tongues? Why would the pastor say he didn't?* Then it hit me like a ton of bricks, *The pastor doesn't know! Wow! Why am I trusting someone to teach me the Bible who doesn't even know that Paul spoke in tongues?* That day, I knew my days at Bethel Baptist Church were numbered.

It has often been said that a man with a testimony will never be at the mercy of a man with an argument. My testimony was just beginning. I began to go to work and ask people, who I knew were Christians, if they spoke in tongues. I found one guy who said his wife did and one guy who said he once did but had backslid. Most people of the Baptist faith strongly discouraged me and warned me to stay away from those Pentecostal doctrines. I was amazed that the Christians whom I worked with had so little knowledge of the Bible. They would make statements without the authority of scriptural knowledge to back them up. I asked one Baptist brother named Ed what he thought about the gift of tongues. He pointed his finger at me and said sternly, "I had a neighbor who was one of them Pentecostals and spoke in tongues, and he backslid and committed adultery!"

It became clear that I was making a lot of believers uncomfortable with my line of questioning. Eventually, I asked Martha, another Baptist lady with whom I had worked, what she thought about tongues. "Dave," she said, "there is a Christian TV station, and they talk about tongues and the Holy Spirit a lot. Maybe they have what you're looking for." She didn't know what channel it was.

Martha had given me hope. I went home that afternoon and went channel-by-channel until I found a station that looked and sounded different than any other station. As I sat and watched, I was amazed. There was an evangelist praying for a sick woman on a cot, and she got up and walked. As he was praying for her, I heard him speak in tongues, and I was hooked. I watched that channel every waking moment. The station was TBN (Trinity Broadcast Network).

One evening, after my wife had gone to bed, I decided to pull the trigger on this issue. I picked up the phone and dialed the 800 number on the screen. A woman answered the telephone, and I asked her if she could explain to me the Baptism of the Holy Spirit. As she spoke, I couldn't understand what she was saying. Finally, I just hung up in frustration.. I sat there and decided to try again. As the phone rang, it was answered by another lady and I said with a little irritation, "Yeah, could you please explain to me what this Baptism of the Holy Spirit and tongues stuff is about?"

This lady began to speak in tongues on the phone and then said, "Sir, the Lord says that He has just delivered you from years of drug addiction and alcoholism, and right now, you need to be on your knees thanking Him. You are going to receive the Baptism of the Holy Spirit and the gift of tongues, but it will be at a time you don't expect it, in a place you don't expect it, and in a way you don't expect it." Then she started praying in tongues again.

I hung up the phone, but I don't remember saying goodbye. I sat there, in a daze, trying to figure out how this lady knew everything about my past and what she meant by everything else she said. I pressed on.

Over the next several weeks, I tried everything I could think of to receive this experience. Nothing seemed to work. Then one night as I again sat in my living room and watched TBN, it started to rain. I got up to look out the window at the streetlight and I heard the guy on TV say, "Now many are going to be healed and many are going to be baptized in the Holy Spirit."

Without any tangible feeling or emotion, I opened my mouth

and began to speak in a language I didn't understand. I stopped and started again and again. *Could this be it?* I wondered. *No, this is too easy,* I finally concluded that if I woke up the next morning and could do it, then it was real!

I awoke the next morning and got into the shower. I was afraid to try to speak because I was afraid I wouldn't be able to speak like I had the night before. *Here we go!* I thought, as I rolled my tongue. Sure enough, this language flowed out of me like water. I was so excited!

After I got to work I found the guy who told me he used to speak in tongues but backslid and didn't do it anymore. I told him what happened and he asked me if I felt anything.

"No," I said.

"Well, that's not it," he answered. I was crushed. He went on to explain how, when he was filled, he had gotten prayer, his whole body tingled, and he felt heat and power surge through him.

Walking away from that conversation, I felt completely vexed with confusion. I began to wonder if I would ever receive this gift, and if it was even for me. I knew I heard the voice of God the day I read Mark 16. He told me, "This is for you son." I did not try to speak in tongues for the next several days.

Then one day ,I decided to get a haircut. I was thinking about a guy who was a barber from the Bethel Church. He had left the church as I did, but I had never known why. I found his shop, walked inside, and began a conversation with him. His name was Gilbert.

"Why did you leave Bethel?" I asked him.

"Well, Dave," he began, "I received the Baptism of the Holy Spirit, and I am going to a little Spirit-filled church now."

I was blown away. "Man, that's what I am looking for," I told him. As we talked, he invited me to come to his church that night and gave me directions. I made it to the service that night and had never seen worship like that. The singers were holding up their hands, and I remember thinking, "Yeah, I see you; You don't have to make such a spectacle out of yourself."

The pastor introduced the guest speaker that night, who had just graduated from Bible College. This would be his first official sermon. The graduate said he didn't know why, but he felt that he was supposed to preach on the Baptism of the Holy Spirit.

I was stoked. As he went through the scriptures, it all made sense. Then came the closing. I believe he thought everyone present was already filled with the Spirit, but he asked if anyone wanted prayer for the Baptism. I jumped to my feet so fast, I scared myself. I went to the front, where the elders gathered around and laid hands on me. I waited for the tingle and heat, but nothing came. They prayed and prayed, but nothing happened.

After what seemed like an eternity, but in reality was only ten minutes, they said, "Well, brother, just believe by faith you have it." I walked out wondering if I was ever going to receive.

I got in my car and just sat there for a minute. "Lord, what am I doing wrong?" I asked silently. As I reached for the ignition and turned the key, I opened my mouth and again that language of the Spirit began to flow just like the night I was looking out my living room window. That was it! I had it! I knew I had it, and no one would ever talk me out of it again!

That was almost thirty years ago, and all I can say is, "Thank God for the wonderful ministry of the Holy Spirit!" After that night, I prayed in my prayer language for hours and hours a day, and my spiritual life accelerated like never before.

I have spent thousands of hours praying in the spirit since that time, and I am here to tell you that there isn't a theological argument from man or devil that will ever convince me that this wonderful experience was not from God. I stand more convinced every day that the Baptism of the Holy Spirit is for every born-again believer. Like many other believers who have experienced the Baptism of the Holy Spirit, I did not experience any tangible physical feeling or manifestation. I want to emphasize this point because many, who are like myself, are being misled, looking for a feeling instead of an experience. As the old saying goes, "Many miss the supernatural looking for the spectacular."

In the following pages, I am going to walk with you through the scriptures and help you understand what this experience is and is not. My prayer is that the Holy Spirit will give you understanding in all things pertaining to His work in the Church. Also, I pray that He will help you to help others, once you are confirmed in this wonderful expression of the love of Christ for His church. After you have experienced the power of the Holy Spirit in your life and ministry, you will understand why Jesus said:

"I came to send fire on the earth, and how I wish it were already kindled! But I have a baptism to be baptized with, and how distressed I am till it is accomplished! Do you suppose that I came to give peace on earth? I tell you, not at all, but rather division.

For from now on five in one house will be divided: three against two, and two against three. Father will be divided against son and son against father, mother against daughter and daughter against mother, mother-in-law against her daughter-in-law and daughter-in-law against her mother-in-law." *Luke 12:49-53*

The Body of Christ still stands divided over this topic. Today, this doctrine will divide the best of friends and closest of family members. But the blessing and benefit of the Gift far outweighs the consequences of any division.

Enjoy the journey!

2
EXPERIENCE

In the parable of the sower, Jesus teaches us that if people do not have an understanding of what they experience or hear being preached, the devil can easily steal that word from them. When people hear others praying in tongues for the first time, and even after they receive the baptism of the Holy Spirit with the gift of tongues for themselves, the devil will immediately begin trying to steal that seed that was planted in their lives.

In that parable, Jesus said that the seed that fell by the wayside was the people who heard the word, but had no understanding. We want to stop that word from being stolen by backing up and explaining everything that God has revealed about the baptism of the Holy Spirit, and the evidence of praying in other tongues.

Many people feel that the experience should be explained before it occurs. However, on the day of Pentecost, the Holy spirit was poured out, and then God explained what had happened after the experience. Peter stood up and explained what happened so that everyone would have understanding. It is important for us as Spirit-filled believers to have a strong knowledge and understanding of this experience so that we can explain it to others who do not have that knowledge.

Why tongues?

Every promise of God can be found in both the Old Testament and the New Testament. I try to show examples from both whenever possible, when I am teaching, so that people can see the parallel between old and new.

Matthew 13:52 "Then He said to them, Therefore every scribe instructed concerning the kingdom of heaven is like a householder who brings out of his treasure things new and old."

When we teach someone out of the Bible, we should be able to show them in the New Testament, and also be able to verify that doctrine in the Old Testament. The new comes out of the old. For example, in Acts chapter 3 it says:

Acts 3:19 "Repent therefore and be converted, that your sins may be blotted out, so that times of refreshing may come from the presence of the Lord."

If we turn to the Old Testament, we can see the parallel in the words of the prophet Isaiah.

Isaiah 28:9-12 "Whom will he teach knowledge? And whom will he make to understand the message? Those just weaned from milk? Those just drawn from the breasts? 10 For precept must be upon precept, precept upon precept, Line upon line, line upon line, Here a little, there a little. " For with stammering lips and another tongue He will speak to this people, "To whom He said, "This is the rest with which you may cause the weary to rest," And, "This is the refreshing"; Yet they would not hear."

I taught this scripture for many years before I had a real understanding of it. In a conversation with a Hebrew scholar years ago, I learned that when verse ten was translated to English, the translators did not know how to interpret it. The correct translation would have used the word *gibberish*, like a baby talking or unintelligible speech.

In other words, God was saying that for Him to teach the people, and them to learn and have understanding, would be like a little kid speaking gibberish. This goes in context with verse nine, a baby drawn from the breast, and verse eleven, stammering lips and another tongue.

In verse twelve, he goes on to speak prophetically, "Yet they still would not hear." This is still being fulfilled in the church today, as a large percentage of the church of Jesus Christ will not lean to the Spirit and away from their own understanding.

Jesus spent much of his ministry rebuking the leaders for taking the knowledge of the word and making it an idol. The word of the Old Covenant had literally become a stumbling block for the nation of Israel. Knowledge puffs up, but godliness profits all. Truth divorced from the Spirit will always create things that God did not intend and produce death in the heart of man.

Luke 11:44-52 "Woe to you, scribes and Pharisees, hypocrites! For you are like graves which are not seen, and the men who walk over them are not aware of them" Then one of the lawyers answered and said to Him, "Teacher, by saying these things You reproach us also." And He said, "Woe to you also, lawyers! For you load men with burdens hard to bear, and you yourselves do not touch the burdens with one of your fingers. "Woe to you! For you build the tombs of the prophets, and your *fathers killed them. ``In fact, you bear witness that you approve the deeds of your fathers; for they indeed killed them, and you build their tombs. "Therefore the wisdom of God also said 'I will send them prophets and apostles". and some of them they will kill and persecute, "that the blood of all the prophets which was shed from the foundation of the world may be required of this generation, from the blood of Abel to the blood of Zechariah who perished between the altar and the temple. Yes, I say to you, it shall be required of this generation. "Woe to you lawyers! For you have taken away the key of knowledge. You did not enter in yourselves, and those who were entering in you hindered."*

This is a very stern warning to religious leaders from Jesus Christ. Today, many men are fulfilling this truth. They have never tasted of the Holy Spirit or His power, yet they are hindering other men from coming into it. A person is not qualified to teach something that they have never experienced.

3
SEEKING

When I was seeking the Holy Spirit as a young man, I kept going to the Baptist bookstore and buying every book I could find about the Holy Spirit and tongues. Every one of them said the same thing -- that it was not for today. They did not give scripture to support this claim, only their own unbelief and religious arguments. We need to be able to teach from experience and the word of God. If you are not saved, you are going to have a difficult time teaching someone else how to get saved.

When God gave men the law under the Old Covenant, they took the law and that power puffed them up. They fell into the trap of pride, and they became corrupted. Jesus had to rebuke the religious leaders and lawgivers because they had misinterpreted

God's will. God set in the New Covenant a safety valve so that those same mistakes would not happen again-- that the knowledge of God would not be taken and used as a weapon to keep people out of the kingdom.

I Corinthians 1:1-18 "For Christ did not send me to baptize, but to preach the gospel, not with wisdom of words, lest the cross of Christ should be made of no effect? For the message of the cross is foolishness to those who are perishing, but to us who are being saved it is the power of God."

You cannot go out on the street today, and walk up to someone who has not been awakened by the Spirit of God, and start telling them how your life has been changed. When you tell them you believe in this invisible person who came to the earth 2000 years ago, they are going to look at you like a crazy person. To them, it is foolishness. What is that going to do to your pride? The biggest reason most people do not witness is because of rejection. This is God's safety valve so the church does not get puffed up.

1 Corinthians 1:19 "For it is written: "I will destroy the wisdom of the wise, And bring to nothing the understanding of the prudent.""

God knew He had to keep us from becoming prideful. How did our King come into the earth? He was born in a barn! How did He come into Jerusalem? He rode in on a donkey! He will come in riding a white horse later, but first He had to bring His people back down to earth.

I Corinthians 1:20-29 "Where is the wise? Where is the scribe? Where is the disputer of this age? Has not God made foolish the wisdom of this world? For since, in the wisdom of God, the world through wisdom did not know God, it pleased God through the foolishness of the message preached to save those who believe. For Jews request a sign, and Greeks seek after wisdom; but we preach Christ crucified, to the Jews a stumbling block and to the Greeks foolishness, but to those who are called, both Jews and Greeks, Christ the power of God and the wisdom of God. because the foolishness of God is wiser than men, and the weakness of God is stronger than men. For you see your calling, brethren, that not many wise according to the flesh, not many mighty, not many noble, are called. But God has chosen the foolish things of the world to put to shame the wise, and God has chosen the weak things of the world to put to shame the things which are mighty; and the base things of the world and the things which are despised God has chosen, and the things which are not, to bring to nothing the things that are, that no flesh should glory in His presence. "

God will use His people to humiliate the world. God will use our salvation, our infilling of the Holy Spirit, our prophecy, and our speaking in tongues, to humiliate the wise. Listen to the prayers of the men who choose education instead of the Spirit-- they are powerless. Most have to write out their prayers and read them as they pray, because they have no unction from the Spirit.

Why do we speak in tongues? Because God has chosen this for us. Why can the church of today not have all of the riches and nobility and respect of the world? Because God has chosen this way to keep us from becoming prideful and corrupt like the Israelites under the Old Covenant. That is why God chose fishermen to go confront religious leaders and why He chose to anoint tax collectors and prostitutes.

I Corinthians 1:30-31 "But of Him you are in Christ Jesus, who became for us wisdom from God -and righteousness and sanctification and redemption- 31 that, as it is written, "He who glories, let him glory in the Lord"

The next time someone tells you that you have a *holier than thou* attitude, or that you think you are righteous, you can tell them that you are. You are righteous, but only through Jesus. Jesus is your righteousness. When the doctors of theology or the wise men of this world come to confront you, you can answer them with this:

I Corinthians 2:1-5 "And I, brethren, when I came to you, did not come with excellence of speech or of wisdom declaring to you the testimony of God. For I determined not to know anything among you except Jesus Christ and Him crucified. was with you in weakness, in fear, and in much trembling. 'And my speech and my preaching were not with persuasive words of human wisdom, but in demonstration of the Spirit and of power, that your faith should not be in the wisdom of men but in the power of God."

I confound the wisdom of men every day. The foolishness of this message confuses worldly men. God chose the foolishness of speaking in other tongues as an evidence of His Holy Spirit upon man.

I Corinthians 2:6-11 "However we speak wisdom among those who are mature, yet not the wisdom of this age nor the rulers of this age, who are coming to nothing. But when I speak the wisdom of God in a mystery, the hidden wisdom which God ordained before the ages for our glory, which none of the rulers of this age knew; for had they known, they would not have crucified the Lord of glory. But as it is written: "Eye has not seen, nor ear heard, Nor have entered into the heart of man the things which God has prepared for those who love Him." But God has revealed them to us through His Spirit. For the Spirit searches all things, yes, the deep things of God. For what man knows the things of a man except the spirit of the man which is in him? Even so no one knows the things of God except the Spirit of God."

How important is it that I receive the Baptism of the Holy Spirit? I can never know anything about God except through the Spirit of God. I can teach people the word of God, but unless the Holy Spirit makes those words alive, in my spirit, they will be forgotten.

I Corinthians 2:12-16 "Now we have received, not the spirit of the world, but the Spirit who is from God, that we might know the things that have been freely given to us by God. These things we also speak, not in words which man's wisdom teaches but which the Holy Spirit teaches, comparing spiritual things with spiritual. But the natural man does not receive the things of the Spirit of God, for they are foolishness to him; nor can he know them, because they are spiritually discerned. But he who is spiritual judges all things, yet he himself is rightly judged by no one. For "who has known the mind of the Lord that he may instruct Him?" But we have the mind of Christ."

God has hidden much wisdom in the word, but the only way to find it is through the Spirit. There is no other way. Why do we need to be Spirit-filled? Because it is the only way to know God. Why should we speak in tongues? Because God has chosen this way for us to relate and communicate more effectively with Him.

4
UNDERSTANDING THE PROMISE

We saw in Isaiah. that it was prophesied. that God would speak to His people with "stammering lips and another tongue." This happened and it is still happening today. Speaking in other tongues was an ordained form of communication between God and His people. It was designed to be a part of your prayer life today.

So many Christians do not believe this, and many believe it, but do not practice it. God promised to pour out His Spirit on anyone who asks at any time. Many Christians are missing out on this promise of God because they lack understanding and they have been taught incorrectly.

Joel 2:28 "And it shall come to pass afterward That I will pour out My Spirit on all flesh; Your sons and your daughters shall prophesy, Your old men shall dream dreams, Your young men shall see visions."

The only qualification listed to experience these gifts is "flesh." It does not say that the Spirit would be poured out only on the people in the upper room, or only on the people that lived during Paul's time. It says, "All flesh." It also says that they shall prophesy-- not that they might prophesy or that some might prophesy. When God pours out His Spirit, people will prophesy, have God-inspired dreams, and see visions.

Joel 2:29 "And also on My menservants and on My maidservants I will pour out My Spirit in those days."

This is a very important scripture because menservants and maidservants were of a very low rank and stature in the community. God included this statement because this outpouring and these gifts do not only apply to apostles or prophets. Everyone can experience these gifts, regardless of their rank, and function in the Gifts of the Holy Spirit.

Joel 2:30-32 "And I will show wonders in the heavens and in the earth: Blood and fire and pillars of smoke. The sun shall be turned into darkness, And the moon into blood, before the coming of the great and awesome day of the Lord it shall come to pass That whoever calls on the name of the Lord Shall be saved."

Anytime someone comes, and tries to argue that the timeframe of the outpouring of the Holy Spirit was only for the early church, this is the scripture to show them. Just as God did not qualify a timeframe for people to be saved, He also did not qualify a timeframe for the flow of the filling of the Holy Spirit. As long as people are being saved, people can be filled with the Holy Spirit.

As Spirit-filled Christians, we need to be able to tell someone how to be filled with the Holy Spirit by showing them in the scriptures. This scripture in Joel is the starting point on a roadmap through the Bible that will direct a person to being filled. If a person starts here, and follows through with the rest of the scriptures in this book, they should be able to answer any questions that arise about being filled with the Holy Spirit.

Matthew 3:11 "I indeed baptize you with water unto repentance, but He who is coming after me is mightier than I, whose sandals I am not worthy to carry. He will baptize you with the Holy Spirit and fire."

Here, John the Baptist is saying, that water baptism is the sign that a person has repented of their sins, but another baptism is needed. Water baptism is good. I believe that every Christian needs to be water baptized. If you were baptized as a baby, and saved as an adult, you should be baptized again, but there is another baptism with the Holy Spirit and fire.

Luke 11: 11-13 "If a son asks for bread from any father among you, will he give him a stone? Or if he asks for a fish, will he give him a serpent instead of a fish? "Or if he asks for an egg, will he offer him a scorpion? "If you then being evil, know how to give good gifts to your children, how much more will your heavenly Father give the Holy Spirit to those who ask Him!"

Some people are afraid to ask God for the Holy Spirit because they think that they will get something else. In fact, I was told as a young boy, that if I asked God to be filled with the Holy Spirit, I would actually receive a demon spirit. I was taught to fear and avoid that experience. I remember the day I found this scripture and was set free from that fear of receiving something evil from God. This scripture shows the nature of God --to give good things to His children when they ask.

This is the reason that Jesus came and died for us. He wants us to be right with the Father and filled with the Spirit. His blood makes us right with the Father, and our faith brings the filling of the Holy Spirit and empowers us for His work on the earth.

Luke 24:46-49 "Then He said to them, Thus it is written, and thus it was necessary for the Christ to suffer and to rise from the dead the third day, 'and that repentance and remission of sins should be preached in His name to all nations, beginning at Jerusalem. 48 "And you are witnesses of these things. Behold. I send the Promise of My Father upon you; but tarry in the city of Jerusalem until you are endued with power from on high."

What is the Promise of the Father? To be endued with power from on high. This was so important that Jesus commanded His disciples to stay in the city, and not go out into the fields to work, until the Promise came. Why? Would you send someone to do a job and then not give them the power to do it? It would be like sending someone out into the inner city to be a policeman, but not giving them a gun. How could a policeman arrest a criminal if he did not have a gun? God empowers us to do the work of the gospel.

So if someone asks, "What is the Promise of the Father?," the answer is, it is "Enduement with power from the Holy Spirit." I would say that most Christians would not know what you were talking about if you asked them about the *Promise of the Father.* People do not know what they are missing when they lack power from on high, when they have not been endued with power.

Mark 16:15-18 And He said to them, "Go into all the world and preach the gospel to every creature. He who believes and is baptized will be saved; but he who does not believe will be condemned. And these signs will follow those who believe: In my name they will cast out demons; they will speak with new tongues; they will take up serpents; and if they drink anything deadly, it will by no means hurt them; they will lay hands on the sick, and they will recover."

He does not say that these signs might follow; He says that they *will* follow. Have you ever heard a parent tell their child that "You *will* clean your room?" I remember being a child and hearing that statement. I knew that meant that I did not have an option.

Most denominations try their best to keep their people away from this page in the Bible. I was in church my whole life growing up and I never heard this preached. That was why I left the church for a while. The church I was attending had no power. My picture of a New Testament Christian was a person who dressed up once a week on Sunday, and watched television the rest of the week. What a boring life! That is not God's idea of a New Testament Christian.

He says they will cast out devils, speak with new tongues, and lay hands on the sick. I like that picture much more than the first!

John 20:21 "So Jesus said to them again, "Peace to you! As the Father has sent Me, I also send you."

The word *as* means *in the same manner*. God sent Jesus with power, which means that we are sent in the same manner — *with power*. What happened before Jesus started His ministry? First, He was baptized by John in the Jordan River, and then the heavens opened and the Holy Spirit came on Him. All of this happened before He went out to do his work. This is the way of God.

John 20:22 "And when He had said this, He breathed on them, and said to them "Receive the Holy Spirit."

Many denominations teach that a person receives the Holy Spirit as soon as they are saved. It is true that the Holy Spirit is the one who brings you in and draws you to salvation, but even after Jesus had spoken to the disciples, breathed on them and told them to receive the Holy Spirit, He told them *not* to leave until they were endued with power. When a person is saved, the Holy Spirit begins the work of regeneration in their spirit, but they are not filled with His power until they receive the Baptism of the Holy Spirit.

Acts 1:4-8 "And being assembled together with them, He commanded them not to depart from Jerusalem, but to wait for the Promise of the Father, "which," He said, "you have heard from Me; for John truly baptized with water, but you shall be baptized with the Holy Spirit not many days from now. "

The next thing that happens is really interesting because even after Jesus gives these instructions, the disciples still get distracted from the Promise.

Acts 1:6-8"Therefore, when they had come together, they asked Him, saying, "Lord, will You at this time restore the kingdom to Israel? And He said to them, "It is not for you to know times or seasons which the Father has put in His authority. "But you shall receive power when the Holy Spirit has come upon you; and you shall be witnesses to Me in Jerusalem, and in all Judea and Samaria, and to the end of the earth. "

The disciples were distracted by other things, but Jesus immediately brought them back to the Promise of the Father. Because Jesus had one thing on His mind. The disciples had all kinds of other things on their minds and kept missing the point, but Jesus kept bringing them back to His purpose — which was the Promise of the Father. The church as a whole minimizes the empowerment. They capitalize on salvation, they capitalize on grace, but they minimize empowerment. The devil is very good at keeping people distracted from the Promise of the Father.

5
SECRET WEAPON

In a military situation, what is the first thing that an attacking army tries to destroy? They go after the big guns -- the powerful weapons, and they try to take out the means for communication. Praying in tongues is a supernatural way of communicating with God, and the devil will do everything he can to disrupt that. When you pray in other tongues, the devil is confounded. He does not know what to do or how to fight against you, because he has no communication in that realm.

Different kinds of tongues are secret weapons of the church. It is the restoration of the one language of the earth that was lost at the tower of Babel. If God can get the church under one language, under the unity of the Spirit, which is the bond of peace, nothing is impossible to them!

The only way we can be in unity and speaking one language, is to pray in tongues because when we pray in other tongues, *no one is praying anything contrary to what another person is praying.* The church can be in perfect unity.

Are the gifts still relevant for today?

Many denominations teach that this is not relevant for our generation, but they are deceived by the devil to believe this, and end up forfeiting a very important advantage -- the Promise of the Father.

Throughout church history, from the experience in the upper room until now, there has never been a time when the Holy Spirit was not moving and His gifts were not being experienced.

Acts 2: 1-6 "When the Day of Pentecost had fully come, they were all with one accord in one place. And suddenly there came a sound from heaven, as of a rushing mighty wind, and it filled the whole house where they were sitting; Then there appeared to them divided tongues as of fire and one sat upon each of them and they were all filled with the Holy Spirit and began to speak with other tongues, as the Spirit gave them utterance. And there were dwelling in Jerusalem Jews, devout men, from every nation under heaven. Now when this was noised abroad, the multitude came together, and were confounded, because that every man heard them speak in his own language."

This passage is very important when you are teaching someone about the Holy Spirit, because it says that they were confused. Many Christians today, take a scripture, like James 3:16, and because of the way it is worded in our modern translations, they use it against the works of the Holy Spirit. The scripture says that where envy and strife exist, confusion and every evil thing are there. Many people take that scripture and say that anything that causes confusion is evil and not of God. Sometimes, people are confused when they first witness the movement of the Holy Spirit, so this scripture is twisted to say that the movement cannot be God.

If you look at the root of the word confusion in Acts versus the root word in James, it becomes clear. In James, the word confusion is actually the word for revolt and rebellion. In Acts, it literally means that they were confused. They were puzzled because all of them heard in their own native language. Anytime you learn something new that contradicts what you believe, your brain will be confused for a period of time. If you know the Bible well, you can overcome that confusion.

Acts 2: 7-12 "Then they were all amazed and marveled, saying to one another, "Look, are not all these who speak Galileans? "And how is it that we hear, each in our own language in which we were born? Parthians, and Medes, and Elamites, and the dwellers in Mesopotamia, and in Judaea, and Cappadocia, in Pontus, and Asia, Phrygia, and Pamphylia, in Egypt, and in the parts of Libya about Cyrene, and strangers of Rome, Jews and proselytes, Cretes and Arabians, we do hear them speak in our tongues the wonderful works of God. And they were all amazed, and were in doubt, saying "What does this mean?"

6
MANIFESTATIONS

The New Testament describes three manifestations of the gift of speaking in other tongues. They are three very distinct operations — praying in tongues to communicate to God in private, giving a message in tongues, which will be interpreted to edify a congregation, and speaking in a tongue in an earthly language that the speaker does not know or does not learn but other people understand. Some people, because they are ignorant of the scriptures, will say that if you speak in tongues but it is not another language of the earth, then you are not operating in the Holy Spirit. Having the ability to speak spontaneously in a language that you never learned and be understood by someone else is only one of the manifestations of the gift of tongues. This way is demonstrated in Acts 2:7-8 when the multitudes heard the disciples speak in their own foreign tongue.

This manifestation only occurs at certain times, and I have only experienced it once in my life. Many years ago, I was praying in tongues and a lady came up to me and said that I was speaking perfect Latin. I had never learned Latin in my life, but the lady had learned it and understood what I was saying. God allowed me to speak in a language that she understood, even though I did not. I have heard many stories similar to mine, but most of the other stories I have heard happened in other countries where a missionary was trying to communicate with native people without an interpreter. It does not happen every Sunday, but it does happen.

Acts 2:13-16 " Others mocking said, They are full of new wine."

Remember, we learned earlier that God used the foolishness of these things to prevent pride in the heart of man. Some people will mock you when you move in the Holy Spirit.

They will throw all sorts of names at you — fanatics, snake-handlers, holy rollers — but you have to remember that God made it this way to prevent pride.

Acts 2:14-16 But Peter, standing up with the eleven, raised his voice and said to them, "Men of Judea and all who dwell in Jerusalem, let this be known to you, and heed my words. "For these are not drunk, as you suppose, since it is only the third hour of the day. But this is what was spoken by the prophet Joel"

Peter stood up to explain to the people what was going on. When the Holy Spirit moves, sometimes it needs to be explained. When the Spirit moves in a service, I like to stand up and explain what occurs, especially if visitors are present.

Acts 2:17-18 "And *it shall come to pass in the last days, says God, That I will pour out of My Spirit on all flesh; Your sons and your daughters shall prophesy, Your young men shall see visions, Your old men shall dream dreams. And on My menservants and on My maidservants I will pour out My Spirit in those days; And they shall prophesy."*

Many people take this scripture against speaking in tongues

because it says "prophesy" and does not specifically say "speak in other tongues." As we go on through the scriptures, we will see that giving a message in tongues with an interpretation, is equal to prophesying in English, so that argument will not work either. Tongues work together with the gift of prophecy.

Acts 2: 19 - 21 "1 Will show wonders in heaven above And signs in the earth beneath: Blood and fire and vapor of smoke. The sun shall be turned into darkness, And the moon into blood, Before the coming of the great and awesome day of the Lord. And it shall comes to pass That whoever calls on the name of the Lord Shall be saved."

Acts 2:32-33 "This Jesus God has raised up, of which we are all witnesses . "Therefore being exalted to the right hand of God, and having received from the Father the promise of the Holy Spirit, He poured out this which you now see and hear."

This confirms, yet again, that the Promise of the Father is the outpouring of the Holy Spirit. We can now walk up to any person on the street and show them scripture after scripture saying that the Promise of the Father is the baptism of the Holy Spirit. The main focus of Jesus' ministry was to get back to heaven so He could send the Holy Spirit and power.

Acts 2:37-39 *"Now when they heard this, they were cut to the heart, and said to Peter and the rest of the apostles, "Men and brethren, what shall we do?" Then Peter said to them, "Repent and let everyone of you be baptized in the name of Jesus Christ for the remission of sins; and you shall receive the gift of the Holy Spirit. For the promise is to* *you* *and to* *your children* *and to* *all* *who are* *afar off* *as many as the Lord our God will call."*(emphasis mine*)*

Who is *you*? Anyone who reads this becomes the *you* in this scripture. It goes on to say that it is to *your children*. That alone disqualifies the statement that the gifts of the Spirit died out with Paul because they had children that lived past the time of Paul. It also says *as many as the Lord our God will call*. Is the Lord still calling people? If He is, then the Holy Spirit is still available.

Galatians 3:13-14 *"Christ has redeemed us from the curse of the law, having become a curse for us (for it is written, "Cursed is everyone who hangs on a tree"), that the blessing of Abraham might come upon the Gentiles in Christ Jesus, that they might receive the* Promise of the Spirit through faith.*"* (emphasis mine)

The Holy Spirit is even available to the Gentiles. I can receive the promise of Abraham, even though I am a Gentile, through Jesus Christ. I can also receive the promise of the Spirit, through faith in Jesus Christ. I am an adopted Jew. I have received the spirit of adoption through Jesus Christ.

Every Christian needs to know this well enough to share it with others. You need to be so fluent in it that it pours out of you like water.

Ephesians 1:13-14 "In Him you also trusted, after you heard the word of truth, the gospel of your salvation; in whom also, having believed, you were sealed with the Holy Spirit of promise, who is the guarantee of our inheritance until the redemption of the purchased possession to the praise of His glory"

Flowing in the gifts of the Holy Ghost is the guarantee of our inheritance, and an evidence of our salvation. How do I know that I have eternal life? I have the guarantee, and this guarantee has no expiration date. When the devil tries to cause me to doubt God, I just pull out my guarantee. I cast down the evil thoughts that the devil tries to put in my mind, and pray in the Holy Spirit. He is my guarantee that I am on the right track.

7
CHALLENGES

When I have been challenged by people from other denominations regarding tongues, they would always bring up 1 Corinthians 13 to try to refute what I believed.

1 Corinthians 13:1-8a "Though I speak with the tongues of men and of angels, but have not love, I have become sounding brass or a clanging cymbal. And though I have the gift of prophecy, and understand all mysteries and all knowledge, and though I have all faith, so that I could remove mountains, but have not love, I am nothing. And though I bestow all my goods to feed the poor, and though I give my body to be burned, but have not love, it profits one nothing. `Love suffers long and is kind; love does not envy; love does not parade itself is not puffed up; does not behave rudely, does not seek its own, is not provoked, thinks no evil, does not rejoice in iniquity, but rejoices in the truth; bears all things, believes all things, hopes all things, endures all things. Love never fails"

Right in the middle of his teaching to the Corinthians, Paul was moved by God to interject this doctrine — *the gifts of the Holy Spirit will not produce on the earth unless the motivation of love is attached to them.* You can speak in tongues, but if you are a mean spirited person, what good is it? You are like a clanging cymbal.

I Corinthians 13:8b-10 "But whether there are prophecies, they will fail; whether there are tongues, they will cease; whether there is knowledge, it will vanish away. For we know in part and we prophesy in part. But when that which is perfect has come, then that which is in part will be done away."

Is the word *will* a past, present or future tense verb? It is future. It says that these things will cease, not that they have ceased. Look at the statement about knowledge. It says that it will vanish away. What is knowledge? The Greek word there is "gnosis" meaning general intelligence. At this present time, has knowledge vanished? I think most people would agree that knowledge has not vanished.

The next time someone from a denomination tells you that tongues have ceased, because in 1 Corinthians 13 it says that tongues will cease, you can just pull out your Bible and show them this scripture and ask if knowledge has vanished.

How can knowledge vanish? You have to look at the definition of knowledge. The word knowledge is fragmentary. It means a part or a piece of the truth. How can it vanish? It can only vanish when we have the whole truth. When we have been given the mind of God, knowledge or *pieces of the truth* will be gone. That will be our state someday. When the Perfect comes, that which is imperfect will be done away with, but it has not happened yet.

Has prophesy ceased? How can it when there are still

prophecies to be fulfilled? Take the book of Revelation, for example. It has not all been fulfilled yet. None of these things have passed away because that which is Perfect has not come yet. If prophecy and knowledge have not vanished or ceased, how can a person pick out tongues and say that it has? Tongues are included with prophecy and knowledge. They have not ceased.

When you take away the religious clichés, and the fear and the false doctrine, people can have their faith restored to receive the Promise of the Father. Why is Satan so intent on distracting people from this? Go back and think about a war. Remember, what would Satan want to attack first? The big guns --the empowerment of the church such as boldness, gifts, and our secret weapon of communication with God. Satan focuses his attack on our power. He wants us to lose that power. When you look at the book of Acts, whenever people were converted to Christ, there was a subsequent manifestation of the Holy Spirit.

Acts 10:44-48 "While Peter was still speaking these words, the Holy Spirit fell upon all those who heard the word. [45] And those of the circumcision who believed were astonished, as many as came with Peter, because the gift of the Holy Spirit had been poured out on the Gentiles˙ also For they heard them speak with tongues and magnify God. Then Peter answered˙ "Can anyone forbid water, that these should not be baptized who have received the Holy Spirit just as we have? And he commanded them to be baptized in the name of the Lord. Then they asked him to stay a few days."

Why were the Jews astonished? For 4000 years, the Jews were the capitalists of the things of God. They were the only nation that was included in the covenants. If you believe something for 4000 years, and then it changes in one moment, you would be astonished too. They were not allowed to eat with Gentiles, they could not marry Gentiles, they could not even bring a Gentile into their house unless they were circumcised first. Now uncircumcised people were receiving the Promise. The Jews had missed all the prophesies of Isaiah about the Spirit coming on the Gentiles. How did they know that the Gentiles had received the Spirit? They heard them speaking in other tongues. They witnessed a physical manifestation of the Holy Spirit. On the Day of Pentecost, they saw cloven tongues of fire over their heads and heard them praying in other tongues. There had to be a physical manifestation of the Holy Spirit upon them, otherwise how would they know that He was there? From this, we can deduct that whenever the Spirit is poured out, there will be a physical manifestation of His presence.

Acts 19:1-2 "And it happened, while Apollos was at Corinth, that Paul, having passed through the upper regions, came to Ephesus. And finding some disciples he said to them, "Did you receive the Holy Spirit when you believed?" So they said to him, "We have not so much as heard whether there is a Holy Spirit."

Why would Paul ask this question of these disciples? Because Paul himself did not receive the Holy Spirit when he believed. Jesus appeared to Paul on the road to Damascus, blinded him, and called Paul to spread His gospel on the earth. Paul accepted Jesus, but he was not at that point Spirit-filled. He prayed and fasted for a couple of days. Then God spoke to another man and told him to go to Paul, lay his hands on Paul that he would receive his sight and be filled with the Holy Spirit. (Acts. 9:17) In other words, the scripture tells us over and over again that the filling of the Holy Spirit comes after salvation, not necessarily at the same time. People can be led into salvation and then right into the filling of the Holy Spirit, but it does not always happen that way.

Acts 19:3-7 "And he said to them, "Into what then were you baptized?" So they said, "Into John's baptism. Then Paul said, "John indeed baptized with a baptism of repentance, saying to the people that they should believe on Him who would come after him, that is, on Christ Jesus." When they heard this, they were baptized in the name of the Lord Jesus. And when Paul had laid hands on them, the Holy Spirit came upon them, and they spoke with tongues and prophesied. Now the men were about twelve in all."

These people had already repented and received John's baptism. But when Paul laid hands on them, they were filled with the Holy Spirit. How do we know that they were filled with the Holy Spirit? They spoke with tongues and prophesied. There is always an outward evidence of the Holy Spirit, and the evidence is not just speaking in tongues. God also wants us to prophesy. If you are Spirit-filled, you have the ability inside of you to prophesy. I have also had people argue and say to me before that there are instances in the Bible where the Holy Spirit came and the people did not speak with other tongues. But look at the following scriptures:

Acts 4:3 "And when they had prayed, the place where they were assembled together was shaken; and they were all filled with the Holy Spirit, and they spoke the word of God with boldness."

People always point out this scripture to me as an example of the Spirit coming without the evidence of speaking in tongues. But who were these people in this scripture? If you go back and read this whole chapter, these were the apostles and their followers who were filled on the Day of Pentecost. They had gone out to different places, and preached the word, and persecution came upon them. So these same people reassembled, and the Spirit of God came upon them, and refreshed them. The Spirit came on them this time with a renewed strength and boldness to speak the word of God without fear.

This shows us another fact about the Spirit. It is not a one-time event. You can be refilled many times. The very word filled means continuously. In other words, the water of God never stops running. We have to be continuously filled. We receive the initial baptism, but then we must remain filled through daily walking with God, daily prayer, daily communion, corporate worship, prayer meetings, and church attendance. These activities help us to remain filled.

8
ADMINISTRATION

1 Corinthians 14:1 "Pursue love, and desire spiritual gifts, but especially that you may prophesy".

The word "desire" means to want something strongly. God wants for us to strongly seek after spiritual gifts, especially prophecy. Many people think that they do not prophesy because they do not stand up in church and give a word. That is not the only way to prophesy. Anytime you preach or teach, that is the spirit of prophesy. If you feel an urge to go tell someone something, to tell someone that God loves them, that is the spirit of prophecy.

Revelation 19:10 says: "For the testimony of Jesus is the Spirit of prophecy..." Prophecy is one of the evidences that you have received The Holy Spirit. I have encountered some believers that say they have never prophesied, prayed in tongues, cast out a devil, or laid hands on the sick. I would have to question whether that person is really filled with the Spirit. There will always be an evidence of the filling of the Holy Spirit. When He comes in you, He comes with a desire. You will be filled with a desire for God. If your Christian life can be described by the word boring, you are not filled with the Holy Spirit. We should greet everyday with expectations for the Spirit to move. Our Christian life should be an adventure.

1 Corinthians 14:2 "For he who speaks in a tongue does not speak to men but to God for no one understands him; however, in the spirit he speaks mysteries."

In the Spirit means *praying in tongues.* Many people often say that a person can be *in the Spirit* and pray in their own language, but you will find that nowhere in the Bible. Every place in the Bible, that refers to praying in the Spirit, makes reference to praying in tongues.

Speaking in tongues is a mystery that only God understands. When a person prays in tongues, his spirit is communing with God in a way that his mind cannot understand, and other men cannot understand. When a person is in the Spirit, he is uncorrupted and perfect. It is a universal language that unites the church. When the church moves out of the Spirit, impossibilities arise, but when the church is in the Spirit, there is perfect unity. When I pray in tongues, it cannot be corrupted by my own understanding or prejudices.

1 Corinthians 14:3 *"But he who prophesies speaks edification and exhortation and comfort to men"*

A prophecy is given to men, in order to edify, exhort, or to comfort. Prophecy is not to God, but to men. Prophecy is an encouragement to people. The devil has a counterpart to this. The devil's counterpart to praying in tongues is cursing, and his prophecy is gossip. His language is used to tear people down; God's language is used to build people up. Also, consider that prophesying and being a prophet are not the same thing. You can prophesy without operating in the office of a prophet. A prophet is a governmental agent in the church, a part of the five fold ministry. But anyone who is filled with the Spirit can edify, exhort, or comfort people.

1 Corinthians 14:4 "He who speaks in a tongue edifies himself but he who prophesies edifies the church"

The gifts were meant for the church. People try to take the gifts out of the church, which is why there are so many discouraged Christians around. They are not receiving their edification. They are not being spiritual. God did not call you to be good; He called you to be spiritual. Speaking in tongues is important because it edifies the person, but that can be done privately. Prophesying is important because it builds up the church. Both are important, but prophecy is more important for the church as a whole.

I Corinthians 14:5 "I wish you all spoke with tongues, but even more that you prophesied; for he who prophesies is greater than he who speaks with tongues, unless indeed he interprets, that the church may receive edification."

We all know that in Christ's kingdom, it is better to give

than to receive. Christ gave His life for us. The Father gave His only begotten Son. Here Paul is further illustrating this principle. It is better to give edification through prophesy than to receive edification through praying in tongues. This does not minimize praying in tongues, this just says it is more important to build up the church than to build up yourself. He is setting a precedent in the church.

This is also an important scripture because it explains tongues with interpretation. If you pray in tongues, and then God gives the interpretation, this is equal to prophecy. Not only is the person edified, but because the rest of the congregation can understand, and they also receive edification.

1 Corinthians 14:6 "But now, brethren, if I come to you speaking with tongues, what shall I profit you unless I speak to you either by revelation, by knowledge, by prophesying, or by teaching?"

Here we see different forms of spiritual communication. I can bring different styles of exhortation to the church. When I preach, sometimes I preach a message of revelation. Sometimes I preach to give knowledge to the people listening, or sometimes my message is of prophetic inspiration. Oftentimes I teach, going scripture by scripture and explaining them as I go.

Even though speaking and praying in tongues is one of the most beautiful gifts that God has given the church, it is also one of the most abused. Many churches abuse this gift, especially the older, more backward sects. They get caught up in the gift of speaking in tongues and they do not use it according to scripture. They do not have interpreters in public worship, they do not use the gift the way the apostle directed us to use it, which causes confusion in the church and brings a reproach on the Holy Spirit instead of glorifying God.

I have been in old Pentecostal churches where someone will jump up right in the middle of preaching and give a long exhortation in tongues. Then they will sit back down, and the preacher will continue preaching. There is no interpretation, and if you ask them about it, they will say that the Spirit moved on them. That is unscriptural. We are able to control what the Spirit of God does inside of us. It is vital that we have an order in the church, otherwise people will think we are crazy. We are here to show people that God is a God of government. His church is called a kingdom. There has to be some control in the church. In the kingdom, there is a balance. People that have been in the charismatic movement will start screaming Jezebel when you say this. Government is not Jezebel; corrupt government is Jezebel. Control is not wrong; personal manipulative control is wrong. Authority is not wrong; abuse of authority is wrong.

1 Corinthians 14:7-11 "Even things without life, whether flute or harp, when they make a sound, unless they make a distinction in the sounds, how will it be known what is piped or played? For if the trumpet makes an uncertain sound, who will prepare for battle? So likewise you, unless you utter by the tongue words easy to understand, how will it be known what is spoken? For you will be speaking into the air. There are, it may be so, many kinds of languages in the world, and none of them is without significance. "Therefore, if I do not know the meaning of the language, I shall be a foreigner to him who speaks, and he who speaks will be a foreigner to me."

In other words, make sure everything you are doing is not for your own personal enjoyment, your own personal edification, or your own personal revival. Make sure what you are doing is for the whole of the body. The Holy Spirit has a corporate flow. God's Spirit starts at the head and goes down. If God is going to move in the Spirit, He will let the person in authority know. God put the ears on the head for a reason both physically and spiritually. I have had people come up to me in a service and tell me that I missed it because God wanted to do something else. I prayed and sought God and God put me in authority over my church. He showed me what He wanted to do. He always shows me the way He is going to move, and then there is a flow to that. You do not go into work and tell your boss how to run a business. Some people will come into a church and have an exalted opinion of themselves. They get in spiritual pride and try to jump God's chain of command and declare what should or should not be done in a service. This does not follow the government, nor the plan of God.

9
POWER UP

You have to connect to a leader with whom you can agree, and work in agreement with them. If you do not agree with the gifts of the Holy Spirit in a kingdom government, you will not be comfortable in my church. You have to find a leader to whom you can connect. *I believe people are called to leaders not buildings or properties.* There are many churches in the land, and God tells you to choose a place to worship where you can submit to the leadership. Every service is not going to be exactly what you want. When you do not agree, you either submit or leave. In a corporate flow, you are following the direction of the leader. That is called a government controlled service. The Spirit can flow, but there has to be some control. If you cannot submit to a leader, it is okay for you to leave. If the leader is corrupt, you need to just leave. Duck and run, like David did from King Saul. If you try to take down the leader, you will be operating under a curse called "touch not my anointed." God is the only one that can take down a leader.

1 Corinthians 14:12 "Even so you, since you are zealous for spiritual gifts, let it be for the edification of the church that you seek to excel."

Spiritual does not need to be weird. This is where God-given common sense must come into play. You can be so spiritual that you no longer edify the church, but you cause division and confusion in the church. You can become too spiritual. By this I mean that you function so abnormally and in such another dimension, that people can no longer accept what you are doing as God because it is so *out there.*

Anytime God pours out His Spirit, it is designed to rekindle the passion in men's hearts. But anytime men connect to one specific manifestation of the Holy Spirit, and try to make that manifestation the only evidence of God's Spirit being there, they always move into error. Too much of any one truth will do this.

I attended a meeting that was an offshoot of the Toronto revival. When we went into the meeting, it was so chaotic that I just had to leave. The people had so capitalized on the manifestation, that they became completely weird. I could not take a normal person into that building and have them understand what was going on there.

For another example, in the 1800's, there was a move of God in Kentucky, and one of the manifestations was that people would begin to jerk. It was a legitimate move of God. Thousands of people came to Christ in that movement, but when God brought that move to an end, the people did not want to let go of that manifestation. You can go into churches today in Southern Ohio and Kentucky, and people will begin to jerk in the middle of the service, but it does not bring God's move. It only brings confusion because God is no longer moving in that manifestation.

When He moves in a manifestation, it produces fruit, revival, and understanding is in it. However, when people take that manifestation and try to duplicate it, confusion comes into the church. It causes complete confusion or distraction from what God is really trying to do. One time, at my church in Jackson, Ohio, we had a five week revival. People were having open visions, angels appeared, and people were drunk in the Spirit for 24 hours at a time. It was an awesome move of God, but at the end of the five weeks, it came to an end. We had been refreshed, and it was time to go back to work. But there were people who did not want to go back to work. They wanted to stay drunk. They began to abuse what had been given as a refreshing by making it an escape from responsibility. We had to pull them aside and correct them. You cannot spend your whole life drunk in the Holy Spirit. It is called a time of refreshing. We are designed to do kingdom business. We have filling stations, but we cannot stay there all the time. You have to *produce fruit, not become a fruit.*

10
MATURING YOUR GIFT

I Corinthians 12:13 "Therefore let him who speaks in a tongue pray that he may interpret."

When your gift grows from praying in tongues, to giving a message in tongues to the corporate body, pray that you may interpret. I interpret tongues all the time, but I am very careful about interpreting my prayer language. My prayer language was not intended for interpretation. It was designed to portray mysteries unto God. But when I speak in tongues in a corporate setting, I know that was designed to be interpreted, so I seek that interpretation. In your private prayer life, be careful that you do not seek an interpretation. The longer you pray in tongues and the more experienced you become, you will start to recognize the different tongue languages. I have a tongue that is for interpretation, and when I hear it, I know that it is one for interpretation. But many of the other tongues in which I pray are just the mysteries of the kingdom. I am making intercession for the saints and it is not to be interpreted. If I try to interpret, I will interpret out of my own heart, and be led into deception.

I Corinthians 14:14-19 "For if I pray in a tongue, my spirit prays, but my understanding is unfruitful. "What is the conclusion then? I will pray with the spirit, and I will pray with the understanding. I will sing with the spirit, and I will also sing with the understanding. otherwise, if you bless with the spirit, how will he who occupies the place of the uninformed say "Amen at your giving of thanks, since he does not understand what you say? For you indeed give thanks well, but the other is not edified. I thank my God I speak with tongues more than you all; yet in the church I would rather speak five words with my understanding, that I may teach others also, than ten thousand words in a tongue."

The Apostle Paul is trying to teach the church to prioritize. Yes, speaking in tongues is vital, important, and enriching. It has a place in your prayer life and in the church. But in the church, it is more important to speak in an understood language so all can understand. When the Spirit begins to move on me or when I am worshipping God, many times I feel an urge to pray in tongues or sing in the Spirit. But when I want to do that, I always stop myself and look around to see if there is anyone who will not understand what I am doing and be offended. I do not want to confuse someone who is uninformed. It is more important to prevent confusion in someone who is uninformed and sing in the understanding, than to take off in tongues and offend someone.

I Corinthians 14:20-22 *"Brethren, do not be children in understanding; however, in malice be babes, but in understanding be mature. In the law it is written: "With men of other tongues and other lips, I will speak to this people; And yet, for all that, they will not hear Me," says the Lord. Therefore tongues are for a sign, not to those who believe but to unbelievers; but prophesying is not for unbelievers but for those who believe."*

If you do not capture the whole meaning of what Paul is saying, you can misunderstand this doctrine. It says do not speak in tongues when the uninformed are around, but then it says that tongues are a sign for the uninformed. *They are a sign if you interpret.* If in a worship service, someone stands up and gives a tongue message and then another interprets, that is a sign for the unbelievers. If the leader of the service gives some kind of explanation, then it becomes a tool to win them to Christ.

I Corinthians 14:23-26 "Therefore if the whole church comes together in one place, and all speak with tongues, and there come in those who are uninformed or unbelievers, will they not say that you are out of your mind? But if all prophesy, and an unbeliever or an uninformed person comes in, he is convinced by all, he is convicted by all. And thus the secrets of his heart are revealed; and so, falling down on his face, he will worship God and report that God is truly among you. How is it then, brethren? Whenever you come together, each of you has a psalm, has a teaching, has a tongue, has a revelation, has an interpretation. Let all things be done for edification."

Everything that is done in a corporate service needs to be

done for edification. That is what we need to guard, and that is why sometimes there has to be correction. Sometimes, I will ask people to wait to give something that God tells them, because it is not in the flow of the service. I will have them come back later when the flow is appropriate for what they have. There is nothing wrong with what they had, it was just intended for a different time in the service. We want to help people develop their gifts. No one is born and raised up as the perfect prophet. They have to hone and refine their gift. If someone has an unction for a gift, they need to submit to the government of the kingdom and learn how to use that gift properly. I preached sermons in the early 90's that I would minister differently now. I have grown since then and learned more. Everyone has to grow, and things need to be done in the corporate flow.

I Corinthians 14:27-29, *"If anyone speaks in a tongue, let there be two or at the most three, each in turn, and let one interpret. [28] But if there is no interpreter, let him keep silent in church, and let him speak to himself and to God. [29] Let two or three prophets speak, and let the others judge."*

Many people do not like that part. They do not want someone

judging what they say. If that is the case, that person is out of order because no one is perfect. The Bible says that we prophesy imperfectly. Even Paul says that we see dimly like looking through smoky glass. We do not always see clearly. Many prophesies are a mixture of God and flesh. We are an earthen vessel, and sometimes that earth muddies the water. People have to grow and develop and make mistakes. You do not throw out the gifts because people make mistakes. You let the people learn from their mistakes and go on.

I Corinthians 14:30-32 "If anything is revealed to another who sits by, let the first keep silent. For you can all prophesy one by one, that all may learn and all may be encouraged. And the spirits of the prophets are subject to the prophets".

This is a very important scripture. If this verse was better remembered and understood, there would be much less deception in the church today. A few certain denominations in the Pentecostal realm have a doctrine that you can only move in the Spirit when the Spirit moves on you. They say that when the Spirit moves on them they have no control over that. That is wrong doctrine — it is not in the Bible. The gifts of the Holy Spirit are under control of the possessor. If you say that you cannot control your gifts, I would question whether you might be under a demonic force. Remember verse 32: *The spirit of the prophet is subject to the prophet.*

I Corinthians 14:33 *"For God is not the author of confusion but of peace, as in all the churches of the saints."*

I am not going to go into the woman issue that Paul addresses in the next several verses because that is a long teaching that would require going through the entire New Testament showing where women were used by God. But I will summarize by saying that women do need to be in subjection to their husbands at home and in the church. However, that does not mean that they are not called to prophesy and preach and teach and move in the Spirit. They are allowed participation in these gifts. If you say that they are not, you contradict half of the New Testament.

11
ARE YOU WILLING?

I Corinthians 14: 37-38 "If anyone thinks himself to be a prophet or spiritual, let him acknowledge that the things which I write to you are the commandments of the Lord. But if anyone is ignorant, let him be ignorant."

Many people will never embrace the full gospel message, they will never receive the Baptism of the Holy Spirit, they will never pray in tongues, and they will never prophesy. They have hardened their hearts and closed their minds. Paul is speaking to these people — if you want to be ignorant, be ignorant. But, to the people who are willing, the gifts of the Spirit are here to embrace.

1

I Corinthians 14:39-40 "Therefore, brethren, desire earnestly to prophesy, and do not forbid to speak with tongues. Let all things be done decently and in order."

If you use the gifts with decency and order, they produce much fruit. If you do them out of order, they will produce confusion and chaos and become detrimental to the growth of the church. Why would God give us gifts that we could abuse? This is why God set government in the house. Responsibility comes with gifting. God allows men the choice of being responsible or irresponsible with the gifts. It is His design. We are free-willed beings. We have the choice to misuse His power and His gifts. If you choose to misuse and abuse His gifts, you have the choice to repent or face the consequences and take the risk of premature death or living under curses.

For many years in America, we have only had the choice of an organized church with no Spirit or a disorganized church with the Spirit. I believe there can be a balance of Spirit and uncorrupted government. We can have both. Bottom line — *you do not have to be weird and goofy to be spiritual*. You can be spiritual and intelligent. You can be spiritual and organized. You can be spiritual and under government. You have to use common sense and wisdom. You can be spiritual and also be administrative. God is.

Do you think there is any chaos in His Kingdom? Chaos is not present in the throne room of heaven. Chaos means absence of government and control. Control scares people because it has been so abused in the past, but you do not correct abuse by disuse. You correct abuse by proper use.

Knowing the Power that God Gave You

In the Old Testament, there was a man named Gideon, and the children of Israel were under a very strong oppression at that time. Every time their fields would get ready to be harvested, the Philistines would come in and steal their harvest. So they started hiding and having secret harvests so that they could get their harvest in before the Philistines could steal it. They had winepresses in the wooded areas where they could hide. Gideon was hiding in the winepress from the Philistines and beating his grain on the threshing floor in the winepress. And an angel appeared to Gideon and said, "Oh mighty man of valor..."

Gideon's response was, to paraphrase, "Who? Me?"

He did not know what he had. Inside of Gideon was a faith born of the heart of God that could lead 300 to overcome the greatest armies on planet earth, but he did not know what he had. He was hiding, not knowing that inside of him was enough faith to deliver his nation and subdue other nations. He had no clue. But guess what? The angel woke him up. The angels need to come and wake up the church of America so they can learn what is on the inside of them. Unto them has been given power to subdue the nations, not in the natural realm but in the spiritual realm. We do not war against flesh and blood but against spiritual darkness in our land by overcoming its influence in our lives. Just as Israel was given supernatural natural gifts, gifts of strength and gifts to fight, we are given supernatural spiritual gifts to fight spiritually. The natural gifts to Israel were given to keep a pure blood line until Christ was born. He had to protect the seed, but today God has given supernatural spiritual gifts to protect the sons. At one time, it was for the seed, but now it is for the sons.

The firstborn Son has multiplied, and now there are many sons and daughters. Supernatural gifts have been given to us to protect the sons and daughters of the almighty God, not against physical adversaries but against the spiritual hosts of wickedness, against the assaulting principalities and powers, against demons and darkness. These gifts are to be celebrated, developed, embraced, and magnified — not minimized, hidden, and subdued from the believers. Whenever Israel would not fulfill her role as a warrior, she would go into captivity. Whenever the church today does not fulfill her role as spiritual warrior, she goes into captivity.

Many in the church have come into captivity in the enemy's camp — in their minds, their hearts, and their emotions. They say, *I can't forgive. I can't love.* They live in hindsight. God has declared in His word in Luke 10:19. that He has given you power over all the power of the evil one and nothing by shall any means hurt you! We do not know what is inside of us.

Like I said before, some people will never accept this. That is not to say that they will not go to heaven. They just will never be able to be used in these ways on the earth. God called them to a higher grace. He did not put all of this in the Bible to be ignored. If you are a born again Christian, Jesus promised that you could have power through the Holy Spirit. Do not give up that promise.

God is still calling people today and the Baptism of the Holy Spirit is still here. Praying in other tongues is a very powerful gift that has been given to every believer if they will just accept that gift. As a Spirit-filled believer, you need to teach others about the power that they have available to them.

12
FINAL THOUGHTS

Since 1982, when I received the Baptism of the Holy Spirit, I have prayed in tongues nearly every day of my life. I have experimented with this phenomenon and tried to learn the benefits of the experience. I have experienced a deeper understanding of the person, nature, and Word of God. I immediately recognized an acceleration and momentum in my walk with God and in the power of my Christian witness. Practically, I like to pray in the Spirit or pray in tongues at least an hour daily. There are times in my life where I have been led to pray in the Spirit even longer.

For a period of several years I would pray in the spirit between three and six hours a day. I have learned that when I pray in the Spirit, situations in my life have a divine thread of destiny. I believe, as I begin each day praying in the spirit, I am interceding and the Holy Spirit is ordering my steps for the day. There is a definite manifestation of peace, and a dimension of spiritual reality that I feel as I pray in the Spirit. It is as if the things of the Kingdom of God make sense and become more real than at other times.

I have at times spent several hours praying in the Spirit and it is as if I become so aware of the spirit realm that I don't want to leave. I guess you could say one of the awesome benefits of praying in the Spirit is that the Kingdom of God moves from the ideal to the real in your life. I believe praying in the Spirit is a doorway into the supernatural realm of the gifts and operations of the Holy Spirit. It is an exercise of faith and manifests as a refreshing and illuminating experience in the presence of God.

On March 20, 2007 ABC news released a special report called; "Speaking in Tongues: Alternative voices in faith." The article was written by Vicki Mabrey and Roxanna Sherwood. In this investigation Dr. Andrew Newberg of the University of Pennsylvania tried to find an explanation for the phenomenon of speaking in tongues. "Newburg used CT scans to look at what happens in the brain's control center when someone speaks in tongues." To his surprise, he discovered the speech control center of the brain actually becomes quiet when a participant prayed in tongues. He was inconclusive on proving that tongues were the language of God, but conclusive that they are *not the language of the human brain.*

It is interesting that the article stated "in earlier studies, he looked at what happens in the brains of Buddhist Monks meditating and Franciscan nuns praying. The results were quite different from what happens in the brains of people speaking in tongues, whose brains he found, went quiet in the frontal lobe – the part of the brain right behind the forehead that's considered the brain's control center. When they are actually engaged in this whole very intense spiritual practice, their frontal lobes tend to go down in activity…It is very consistent with the kind of experience they have, because they say they are not in charge. Whatever is coming out of their mouth - they are not not purposefully or willfully trying to do. And that's in fairly stark contrast to the people like –Buddhist Monks and Franciscan Nuns—in prayer, because they are very intensely focused and in those individuals the frontal lobes actually increase in activity."

Well, science has proven what Spirit filled believers have said for 2000 years, *It's not me!* It's the Holy Spirit working in my spirit giving me the utterance. Once again, the reality of God has been proven by science. I don't need an MRI to know, that when I pray in the Spirit, it is not formulated in my brain through a natural process. But for the skeptical believer who has been schooled in unbelief, and heard the erroneous arguments of denominational interpretations of scripture, it may be a deciding factor in letting go of natural reasoning and taking a leap of faith into the supernatural experience in Christ.

It was not the laws of gravity or buoyancy that convinced Peter to leave a boat and walk on water, and it was not an inability of God to keep him afloat when he began to sink. It was faith that caused him to walk and unbelief that caused him to sink.

The scripture says that, *we walk by faith and not by sight* or you could say we move by what we believe in our heart is God's will and not by what our five senses, natural reasoning, or intellectual arguments tell us. I'm finishing another book at this present time entitled: "They Said It Couldn't Be Done". That would describe everything I have done since being filled with God's Holy Spirit. Lester Sumrall, our Commencement speaker, charged our graduating class during Bible College Graduation: "Don't do anything that's possible, if it's possible you don't need God!" I have lived in the realm of impossible since 1982, and will continue to live that way until Jesus comes for me or I go to Him!

If you would like more information on the wonderful ministry of the Holy Spirit, I would like to invite you to our website where you will find archived sermons, healing testimonies and books to purchase for aiding you in the understanding of the Kingdom of God, and the work of the Holy Spirit on the Earth. You can find us at: www.liveattherock.com.

ABOUT THE AUTHOR

David Chisholm was born in Jackson Ohio in 1959. After serving in the US Army and beginning a career in Aviation David met Jesus Christ and experience a radical transformation of life and calling into the ministry. After completing his initial Bible College training and working in Prison Ministry for 3 years, David was directed to plant a non-denominational church in his home town and served as Senior Pastor there for 14 years. In 2000 David again was directed by the Lord to plant another church in Parkersburg, West Virginia, where he presently resides and serves as the Senior Pastor and Apostle over four Rock Family Worship Centers.

David has a unique insight into the operation and manifestation of the Holy Spirit and has been used by God to train many leaders in the ministry. He has a communication style that is direct and insightful as well as an ability to teach the reality of the presence of God that should be experienced in the Church. David's passion is to see the life of the believer come out of the "ideal" and into the "real." David believes it is the Lord's desire for every believer to discover their "gift package" and is committed to helping those who hunger for more of God's person and presence to find and develop their calling.

Other Books by Dr. Chisholm:

The Supernatural Life
Blinded By the Familiar

Made in the USA
Columbia, SC
05 August 2017